DUE DATE	BRODART	09/99	19.95

AMERICAN WRITERS
OF THE
20TH CENTURY

Collective Biographies

AMERICAN WRITERS OF THE 20TH CENTURY

Carmen Bredeson

ENSLOW PUBLISHERS, INC.

44 Fadem Road	P.O. Box 38
Box 699	Aldershot
Springfield, N.J. 07081	Hants GU12 6BP
U.S.A.	U.K.

Library of Congress Cataloging-in-Publication Data

Bredeson, Carmen.
    American writers of the 20th century / Carmen Bredeson.
       p. cm. — (Collective biographies)
    Includes bibliographical references and index.
    Summary: Describes the personal lives and professional accomplishments of ten
American authors of the twentieth century including John Steinbeck, William
Faulkner, Toni Morrison, Maya Angelou, and Ernest Hemingway.
    ISBN 0-89490-704-2
    1. Authors, American—20th century—Biography—Juvenile literature.
[1. Authors, American.] I. Title. II. Series.
PS129.B73 1996
810.9'005—dc20
[B]   95-34790
                                              CIP
                                              AC

Printed in the U.S.A.

10 9 8 7 6 5 4 3 2

Illustration Credits:
Akron Beacon Journal, p. 82; AP/Wide World Photos, p. 76; Courtesy of
Mississippi Department of Archives and History, pp. 60, 66; Courtesy of Paul
Porter, pp. 18, 24; Courtesy of Princeton University; photo by Maria Mulas,
p. 84; F. Scott Fitzgerald Papers, Manuscript Division, Department of Rare
Books and Special Collections, Princeton University, p. 26; Library of Congress,
pp. 45, 68; Moorland-Spingarn Research Center, Howard University Archives,
p. 88; National Archives, pp. 32, 34, 40, 42, 52, 73; The Valley Guild, p. 58;
Willa Cather Pioneer Memorial, Red Cloud, Nebraska, pp. 10, 15.

Cover Illustration:
John Steinbeck and his dog, Charley, 1963
Photograph by Hans Namuth
©1991 Hans Namuth Estate.
Courtesy, Center for Creative Photography
The University of Arizona.
Special permission has been given by the copyright holder
for the image to be cropped from the original photograph.

Contents

Preface

Author James Baldwin once said, "Don't describe it, show it. That's what I try to teach all young writers. . . . Don't describe a purple sunset, make me see that it is purple."[1]

All of the writers included in this book had the fantastic ability to draw pictures for their readers. Unlike other artists, who may use paint, or a piano, or a lump of clay, writers use a string of letters to paint their masterpieces. Their words create scenes that dance in the mind, scenes that can make us laugh with joy or shed tears of sorrow. When they are very good, as are the writers in this book, they can take us away for a little while, to another place and another time.

We may travel with Willa Cather to a windswept Nebraska plain, where pioneers struggle to survive in a harsh environment. Or we might lose ourselves in the wonderful world of John Steinbeck's *Cannery*

Row, where Doc is king and the bums, his lords. Maya Angelou can make us cry as we explore her childhood, and read of the pain and fear one small girl was forced to endure. Ernest Hemingway gives to the reader the danger and excitement that were such a necessary part of his life.

America can lay claim to many talented writers, and the ten in this book are only a representative selection of the very best. These twentieth-century authors started early to practice the art of words. As children, they were voracious readers and listed books as among their favorite things. They learned that within the pages of a book, there were friends to meet and worlds to explore. As they grew older and developed their own craft, they began to provide new worlds for others to investigate. On the pages of their creations they offer to us a chance to live through their eyes.

Many of these authors received recognition and awards for their imaginative and moving works. The Nobel Prize for literature was awarded to William Faulkner (1949), Ernest Hemingway (1954), John Steinbeck (1962), and Toni Morrison (1993). The Nobel Prize has been given annually since 1901, to persons who have made the most significant contributions in the fields of chemistry, medicine, physics, literature, and peace. The monetary awards are funded by a trust that was established in the will of Alfred B. Nobel, who died in 1896.

The Pulitzer Prize is awarded annually to American

authors in the fields of journalism and letters. While the Nobel Prize is given for an entire body of work, the Pulitzer is awarded for a specific piece of writing. The award is funded from the estate of the late Joseph Pulitzer and is given for journalism, fiction, United States history and biography, drama, and poetry. The following authors from this collection were awarded Pulitzer Prizes for fiction:

1923—Willa Cather for *One of Ours*
1940—John Steinbeck for *The Grapes of Wrath*
1953—Ernest Hemingway for *The Old Man and the Sea*
1955—William Faulkner for *A Fable*
1963—William Faulkner for *The Reivers*
1966—Katherine Anne Porter for *The Collected Stories of Katherine Anne Porter*
1973—Eudora Welty for *The Optimist's Daughter*
1988—Toni Morrison for *Beloved*

While many of the authors in this book were successful and popular writers, some of them experienced difficulties in their personal lives. Unhappy childhood is a common thread that links Maya Angelou and James Baldwin. Alcohol and bouts of depression were present in the lives of F. Scott Fitzgerald, Ernest Hemingway, and John Steinbeck. The three African-American writers in this book struggled to be heard during a time of emerging civil rights.

In most cases, events surrounding the daily lives of the authors played a major role in the development of their literature. They drew on their own past experiences and emotions to develop and create their fictional characters. The writers have changed names and locations, but their perceptions remain a vital part of each and every story.

Willa Cather

Willa Cather
(1873–1947)

In 1921, when Willa Cather was forty-eight years old, she said that the "years from eight to fifteen are the formative period in a writer's life, when he unconsciously gathers basic material."[1] For her, those childhood years were filled with memorable experiences that helped to shape and define all of her future writing. The people that she met on the stark and windswept Nebraska prairie would become the characters in her books. Their lives would be embellished to create wonderful tales of hardship and courage, disaster and triumph.

Willa Cather was not born in Nebraska, the setting for her most famous books. She was born in Back Creek Valley, Virginia, on December 7, 1873. She was the first of Charles and Mary Cather's seven children.

The countryside around the Cathers' Virginia home was lush and green, dotted with scenic hills and valleys.

When Willa was nine years old, her world changed dramatically. Charles and Mary Cather decided to uproot their growing family and move to Nebraska to become homesteaders. As the family set out, Willa watched the only home that she had ever known slowly disappear into the distance. The year was 1883, and the Cathers were heading west, along with thousands of other families. Vast, unsettled prairie lands were available for anyone who had the stamina and courage to homestead. Many were drawn to the untamed wilderness and its promise of a new life. The Cathers' destination was the farm of Charles Cather's parents, located near the Kansas-Nebraska border.

As the small band of settlers crossed the heartland of America, the scenery slowly changed. Gone were the green hills and valleys of Virginia. They were replaced by dry, flat plains, barren of all vegetation except for waving prairie grasses. Willa Cather later described her feelings after the family's arrival at her grandparents' farm: "I felt a good deal as if we had come to the end of everything."[2]

The strangeness slowly wore off, and Willa started to explore her surroundings. She roamed all over the countryside, sometimes on her pony and other times on foot. Willa met other families that lived on nearby farms. Many of them were immigrants from Norway, Sweden, and Germany. Willa watched as the immigrant families practiced customs that were unknown to Americans, and listened to their stories about life in faraway lands. She said that when she returned to her home, "their stories used to go round and round in my head at night."[3]

Life on the great western plains of America was rarely easy for the early settlers. Many lived in hastily constructed sod huts that were hollowed out of the hills. Others built small, temporary houses and dreamed of prosperity and larger homes in the future. Winters could be deadly as blizzards ripped across the flat land and pelted the farms with sleet and snow.

Many of the immigrants faced terrible hardships, but they were a hardy and determined people. Willa Cather saw the strength and pride in many that she met on the Nebraska prairie, and their stories remained with her. She later said, "I knew every farm, every tree, every field in the region around my home and they all called out to me. My deepest feelings were rooted in this country."[4]

After a year on the farm, Willa's father decided to move his growing family into the nearby town of Red Cloud, Nebraska, where he opened an insurance and real estate business. After they had settled into their new home, the Cather children were enrolled in school for the first time. Always before, they had been tutored by their maternal grandmother. Willa attended Red Cloud High School and was given private lessons in Greek and Latin by a local store owner.

In 1891, at the age of sixteen, Willa Cather enrolled in the University of Nebraska, in Lincoln. Her writing was first published during her college years. Willa Cather became the literary editor of a school magazine, *The Hesperian,* and many of her early stories appeared in its pages. In 1893, while she was still a college student, Cather was hired by the *Nebraska State Journal* to review plays. She was paid a dollar for each column that was printed in the newspaper.

After her graduation in 1895, Willa Cather had a number of jobs working for magazines and newspapers. In 1901, she moved to Pittsburgh, Pennsylvania, and she taught high school there until 1906. *April Twilights,* Willa Cather's only book of poems, was published in 1903. Two years later, her first book of short stories, *The Troll Garden,* was published.

In 1906, Cather moved to New York City to work as an editor for *McClure's* magazine. Just two years later, she was named managing editor of the magazine, a position she held for three years. After the magazine was sold to a new owner, Cather decided to devote all of her time to writing. Her first novel, *Alexander's Bridge,* was published in 1912. Unlike her later books about the Nebraska prairie, *Alexander's Bridge* was concerned with sophisticated society in Boston and London.

In 1913, Willa Cather wrote her first book about the Nebraska prairie that she had known as a child. The images of immigrants and hardship, stamped onto her child's mind so long ago, once again surfaced

Willa Cather's bedroom in Nebraska has been restored. The original wallpaper that Cather herself bought is still on the walls.

on the pages of *O Pioneers!* She said about the novel:

> I had searched for books telling about the beauty of the country I loved, its romance, the heroism and strength and courage of its people that had been plowed into the very furrows of its soil and I did not find them. And so I wrote *O Pioneers!* [5]

The story tells of Alexandra Bergson and how she must assume responsibility for the family farm after the death of her father. Just before his death, John Bergson calls his children to his bedside and says, "Boys . . . I want you to keep the land together and to be guided by your sister. . . . Alexandra is the oldest, and she knows my wishes. She will do the best she can." [6] Alexandra, like many of Cather's heroines, seems to be far more capable than the men around her. She is also deeply devoted to the land and is rewarded with increasingly good harvests through the years.

My Ántonia, published in 1918, is considered by many to be Willa Cather's finest book about the Nebraska wilderness. It is a story told by Jim Burden as he looks back at his childhood friendship with Ántonia Shimerda. Ántonia must work hard to help her immigrant family make a living on their farm, but still she can laugh and enjoy herself.

When he recalls the early days of their acquaintance, Jim Burden says:

> Ántonia had opinions about everything, and she was soon able to make them known.

Almost every day she came running across the prairie to have her reading lesson with me. Mrs. Shimerda grumbled, but realized it was important that one member of the family should learn English.[7]

Ántonía faces many difficulties during her life, but she has the strength and determination to overcome them and to find joy in what she has.

Willa Cather went on to write nine more novels in addition to her short stories and poems. Often, her characters experienced conflicts between their lives and the environment around them. She never forgot the sturdy and patient immigrants that she knew as a child; she told their stories over and over, writing of their harsh existence on the Nebraska frontier.

Willa Cather lived in New York City during her later years. After her own mother's death in 1931, she never returned to Red Cloud, yet the land that she loved lives on in her books. Willa Cather died on April 24, 1947, in New York City. She once wrote, "We come and go, but the land is always here. And the people who love it and understand it are the people who own it—for a little while."[8]

Willa Cather owned a little piece of American history. By recording her memories of that special time in our country's past, she also gave us a taste of that history. If a writer can bring to life a period or event for those who follow, that is indeed a great accomplishment.

Katherine Anne Porter

2

Katherine Anne Porter
(1890–1980)

At the age of six, Katherine Anne Porter wrote her first novel. She called it *A Nobbel—The Hermit of Halifax Cave.* That early experience at storytelling would be the beginning of a lifelong journey into the world of writing. The journey was seldom easy, but the hardships that she suffered seemed to enhance her works.

On May 15, 1890, Katherine Anne Porter was born in Indian Creek, Texas, a small town located near San Antonio. When she was just two years old, her mother, Mary Alice Porter, died. After the death of his wife, Harrison Porter gathered up his four small children and moved to his mother's house in Kyle, Texas. Katherine's grandmother, Catherine Anne Skaggs Porter, was known to all in the family as Aunt Cat.

19

Aunt Cat was a strong and capable woman who had raised nine children of her own. When her grieving son arrived with his four little ones, she made room for them in her four-room house. Harrison Porter did not contribute much to the family, either in terms of money or guidance. That responsibility fell to Aunt Cat.

Even though the Porters had few belongings, they had a rich source of entertainment in their lives. Aunt Cat was an excellent storyteller, and she regaled her grandchildren with wonderful tales. For nine years, Katherine Anne watched and listened to her grandmother, and she began to develop her own storytelling ability. The young girl also wanted to be an actress and often produced plays in the front yard. Years later, Porter said about her grandmother, "She was really somebody and I'm glad I knew her."[1]

In 1901, when Katherine Anne was eleven years old, her grandmother died. Harrison Porter sold his mother's property and moved the family to San Antonio, Texas. Katherine Anne and her older sister, Annie Gay, were sent to the Thomas School. Katherine said, "I was mad about history, grammar, world geography, music, poetry, painting; I'd put books on subjects that enchanted me inside textbooks and read, read, read."[2] Because her mind was continually lost in stories, Katherine Anne was not a good student, and she remained at the Thomas School for only one year.

Harrison Porter was barely able to support his

children in San Antonio, so once again the family moved, this time to Victoria, Texas. Thirteen-year-old Katherine Anne and Annie Gay opened a studio in Victoria and taught music and drama.

In 1906, when she was just sixteen years old, Katherine Anne Porter met and married John Henry Koontz. This was the first of Porter's four unsuccessful marriages. At the age of twenty-three, Katherine Anne Porter left her husband and moved to Chicago, Illinois, where she worked as an extra in the movies. Because she could not make a living as an actress, Porter returned to Texas in 1914.

Porter's year in Chicago had been hard on her health. Poor nutrition and the effects of a cold climate made Porter ill. She contracted tuberculosis (TB), a contagious lung disease, which was diagnosed upon her return to Texas. At that time there was no treatment for TB, and patients were often sent to sanatoriums for several years to rest and recover. During her time in a sanatorium, Porter met a fellow patient who owned a newspaper in Fort Worth. After Porter's recovery, she began work as the drama critic and society columnist for the *Fort Worth Critic*. A year later, in 1918, she went to Denver, Colorado, to work for the *Rocky Mountain News*.

During her year in Denver, Porter contracted influenza and nearly died. She later used the experience of the influenza epidemic as a basis for her short story "Pale Horse, Pale Rider." After her recovery, she moved to Mexico, where she taught dance at several girls' schools and wrote magazine articles. In 1922, she moved to New York City and wrote "María Concepción." This story, which takes place in Mexico, was Porter's first important piece of fiction.

In the story, eighteen-year-old María's reaction is described after she sees her husband, Juan Villegas, with another woman: "María Concepción did not stir nor breathe for some seconds. Her forehead was cold, and yet boiling water seemed to be pouring slowly along her spine."[3] María decides not to confront her husband, and "found herself walking onward, keeping the road without knowing it, feeling her way delicately, her ears strumming. . . ."[4]

After the publication of "María Concepción," several years would pass before any more of Katherine Anne Porter's works appeared in print. In an interview, she said:

> I made no attempt to publish anything until I was thirty, but I had written and destroyed manuscripts quite literally by the trunkful. I spent fifteen years wandering about, weighed horribly with masses of paper and little else.[5]

In 1930, *Flowering Judas*, Katherine Anne Porter's first collection of short stories, was published. It was a critical success and helped to establish her reputation as a legitimate and serious writer. Porter continued her nomadic life, living for a time in Mexico, Germany, France, and the United States. She taught at Stanford University, and at the University of Michigan.

In addition to her teaching duties, Porter traveled around the country, lecturing and conducting writing seminars. Her three marriages, between 1926 and 1942, all ended in divorce. She once said that she had to be alone in order to write, and that her husbands felt neglected during those times.[6] Porter often would retreat to a hotel room and close herself up for days in order to create her stories.

One of her biographers, George Hendrick, wrote about Porter, "No matter whether she has written about Mexicans, Texans, Irishmen, or Germans, one feels that she knows the people and their backgrounds perfectly."[7] Katherine Anne Porter once said, "My whole attempt has been to discover and understand human motives, human feelings." She added that "I have never known an uninteresting human being, and I have never known two alike."[8]

Porter carefully observed the people around her and used their personalities and lives as a basis for many of her characters. During a twenty-seven-day ocean voyage from Mexico to Germany in 1931, she gathered the material for her only full-length novel, *Ship of Fools*. Published in 1962, thirty-one years after the actual voyage, *Ship of Fools* was an immediate success and became a best-seller.

The novel revolves around the lives of forty people aboard a ship that is bound for Germany:

> On the second evening out from Havana, with twenty-odd days to go, the ship's commissary began doling out the modest

23

Katherine Anne Porter continued to travel and lecture well into her eighties. Here she is shown on her eighty-fifth birthday.

pastimes and amusements of the voyage in the attempt to make life on shipboard resemble a perpetual children's party on land.[9]

The character of David Scott in *Ship of Fools* is based on David Pressly, Porter's third husband.

Most critics gave the book positive reviews. Just one month after its release, Porter sold the movie rights to *Ship of Fools* for $500,000. For the first time in her life, Porter had money; she was seventy-two years old, but she had never had an income that allowed her to live as she wished.

The Collected Stories of Katherine Anne Porter, a group of her previously written stories, was published in 1965. The volume won both a Pulitzer Prize and the National Book Award for Porter in 1966.

With her future financially secure, Katherine Anne Porter finally could relax. In 1969, she said, "I love life, and I've enjoyed it and lived a great deal."[10] When asked how she had spent her free time, Porter replied, "I studied cooking, and music, and grew flowers when I had the chance, and read and listened to music, and enjoyed talk with friends."[11]

Katherine Anne Porter continued to travel and lecture until she had several strokes in 1976. Four years later, in 1980, she died at the age of ninety. Katherine Anne Porter was buried next to her mother in Indian Creek, Texas. Porter had been a careful observer of the people around her and had spent her life learning about the workings of the human spirit.

F. Scott Fitzgerald

F. Scott Fitzgerald
(1896–1940)

Francis Scott Key Fitzgerald was born into a home filled with sorrow. Just months before his birth on December 24, 1896, his parents, Edward and Millie Fitzgerald, lost their two little daughters to illness. Millie Fitzgerald, still filled with grief, viewed every sign of illness in her son with concern.

As a child, Scott was often indulged. He once sent invitations to his seventh birthday party, and none of the guests came. In an attempt to ease his disappointment, Mrs. Fitzgerald allowed Scott to eat his entire birthday cake.

The Fitzgerald family lived in St. Paul, Minnesota, during most of Scott's childhood. Edward Fitzgerald was a rather weak man who was descended from an old and aristocratic southern family. Millie

Fitzgerald's ancestors had come to the United States from Ireland. She was an unusual character who often could be seen wearing shoes that did not match. One biographer wrote, "Fitzgerald inherited his elegance and propensity to failure from his father, his social insecurity and absurd behavior from his mother."[1]

Scott received his early education at St. Paul Academy in Minnesota and the Newman School in New Jersey. When it was time to go to college, he chose Princeton University, in Princeton, New Jersey. As a college student, Scott sought out the most influential students for his friends and belonged only to the best clubs. He once wrote that Princeton was "the pleasantest country club in America."[2]

Scott Fitzgerald seemed to enjoy his time at Princeton thoroughly, but he had to leave the university in 1917 after failing to pass his courses. Fitzgerald's immediate future was decided for him with the entry of the United States into World War I. He joined the army as a second lieutenant and began basic training. As he left his college days behind, F. Scott Fitzgerald said, "I want to be one of the greatest writers who ever lived."[3]

During army training in Alabama, he began to work on a novel, *This Side of Paradise.* In addition to writing, Fitzgerald occupied many of his leisure hours with Zelda Sayre, a beautiful young woman who lived in Montgomery, Alabama, near the army base. Zelda wanted to be a professional dancer. Scott and Zelda fell in love and were engaged to be married.

When Scott Fitzgerald was discharged from the army in 1919, he moved to New York City and worked as a copywriter in an advertising agency. He did not earn a very good salary, much to Zelda Sayre's dismay, and she broke off their engagement. In despair, Fitzgerald began to drink heavily and decided to return to St. Paul to finish his novel. Years later, he recalled, "That novel, begun in a training camp late in the war, was my ace in the hole. I had put it aside when I got a job in New York, but I was . . . constantly aware of it." He added, "If I stopped working to finish the novel, I lost the girl."[4]

Fitzgerald completed his novel and sent the manuscript to several publishers. While he waited to hear from them, he worked for the railroad. When he was notified that a large publishing house wanted to publish his book, Fitzgerald said, "That day I quit work and ran along the streets, stopping automobiles to tell friends and acquaintances about it."[5] One month after *This Side of Paradise* was published in 1920, F. Scott Fitzgerald and Zelda Sayre were married.

Fitzgerald's first book is about a spoiled young man who attends Princeton and becomes involved in literary activities and romance. It is a largely autobiographical work that parallels Fitzgerald's own life. Many of the characters in his first and succeeding books are obsessed with money, power, and glamour, just as Scott and Zelda were.

The couple lived for a time in New York City and made their first trip to Europe in 1921. After their European tour, the Fitzgeralds returned to St. Paul, Minnesota. Scott finished his second novel, *The Beautiful and Damned,* a story about Anthony Patch and his beautiful wife, Gloria. He describes the young couple's lifestyle:

> Having danced and splashed through a lavish spring, Anthony and Gloria found that they had spent too much money and for this must go into retirement for a certain period.[6]

Like Anthony and Gloria in the story, the Fitzgeralds also took an occasional break from their active social life. During one such hiatus, while they were in Minnesota, their only child, Frances (nicknamed "Scottie"), was born. Soon after her birth, however, the Fitzgeralds returned to their glamorous life in New York. They spent much of their time attending wild parties, drinking, and spending money. Even though Scott Fitzgerald earned a lot of money in 1923, he and his wife spent most of it. Fitzgerald made a large part of the family's money writing stories for two popular magazines, the *Saturday Evening Post* and *Scribner's.*

Scott Fitzgerald became a self-proclaimed spokesman for the post–World War I era, which he called the Jazz Age, and reported on the manners and temperament of the times. The hectic search for fun and excitement that affected many in postwar America served as a basis for many of his stories. Scott and Zelda Fitzgerald were among the noisy partygoers who tried to live it up during the period that is often called the Roaring Twenties. The decade was famous for Prohibition and bootleg whiskey, along with gangsters and lawlessness.

As did many other writers and artists in America, the Fitzgeralds made their way to Europe during the 1920s. They lived on the French Riviera and in Paris, and they kept company with other expatriate Americans, such as Ernest Hemingway. Here, Fitzgerald wrote what many consider to be his best work, *The Great Gatsby.* In the story, Jay Gatsby strives to make a fortune in order to win the girl of his dreams. Gatsby's lavish lifestyle is described by Nick Carraway, who lives next door. "There was music from my neighbor's house through the summer nights. In his blue gardens men and girls came and went like moths among the whisperings and the champagne and the stars."[7]

Eventually, alcohol began to take its toll on Scott and Zelda Fitzgerald's mental and physical health. After several suicide attempts, Zelda Fitzgerald was admitted to a clinic in Switzerland. In a letter to Zelda at this time, Scott Fitzgerald wrote, "We ruined ourselves."[8]

After Zelda Fitzgerald was discharged from the clinic, the family returned to the United States to live in Alabama, near Zelda's family. Both Scott and Zelda Fitzgerald were in and out of the hospital several times. He was treated for alcoholism and tuberculosis, and she was treated for psychiatric problems.

F. Scott Fitzgerald and his wife, Zelda, had only one child, a daughter they called "Scottie."

In 1934 at the age of thirty eight, Fitzgerald published *Tender Is the Night*, a story about psychiatrist Dick Diver and his patient, Nicole Warren, who fall in love and marry. The development of their attraction is explored in a scene that takes place early in their relationship:

> He was enough older than Nicole to take pleasure in her youthful vanities and delights, the way she paused fractionally in front of the hall mirror on leaving the restaurant, so that the incorruptible quicksilver could give her back to herself.[9]

Fitzgerald's final book was *The Last Tycoon*. Even though it was never completed, an edition including Fitzgerald's notes for the final chapters, was published in 1941. He was working on it when, in November 1940, he suffered a heart attack that left him very weak. Just a few weeks later, on December 24, 1940, he had another heart attack, and he died soon afterward. He was forty-four.

F. Scott Fitzgerald once wrote that "All the stories that came into my head had a touch of disaster in them—the lovely young creatures in my novels went to ruin, the diamond mountains of my short stories blew up. . . ." Many of Fitzgerald's characters were trapped in self-destructive lifestyles. The tragedy lies in the fact that their creator did not discover a way to halt the destruction of his own life.[10]

William Faulkner

William Faulkner
(1897–1962)

When William Faulkner was asked what he talked about to his neighbors in Oxford, Mississippi, he replied, "The people I know are other farmers and horse people and hunters, and we talk about horses and dogs and guns and what to do about this hay crop or this cotton crop, not about literature."[1] Literature was exactly what William Faulkner created from the everyday lives of the people that he associated with in the small Mississippi town.

William Cuthbert Falkner was born in New Albany, Mississippi, on September 25, 1897, the first of Murry and Maud Falkner's four sons. (He would later change the spelling of his last name to Faulkner.) When William was still a baby, his parents moved to Oxford, Mississippi, in Lafayette County.

The Falkners were descended from a powerful and well-to-do southern family that had been financially ruined by the Civil War.

As a child, William played with his brothers, his cousins, and the servants' children. He liked to ride horses, in spite of the fact that they threw him often, and he played golf and tennis fairly well. During his high school years, he was the quarterback for the football team. William Faulkner was not a successful student. He left Oxford High School in 1914, without earning a diploma.

In 1917, after the United States entered World War I, Faulkner tried to enlist in the army. He was turned down because at five feet five inches tall, he was too short. Instead, he joined the Canadian Air Force, but the war ended before he saw any active duty. He returned to Oxford for a time, and then he enrolled in the University of Mississippi. At that time, military veterans were allowed to go to college even if they had not graduated from high school.

In addition to attending classes in college, William Faulkner also served as postmaster, running the school post office. Faulkner eventually quit the post office job, stating that he did not want "to be at the beck and call of every itinerant scoundrel with 2 cents to invest in a postage stamp."[2] After he received a D in English class and equally dismal grades in his other classes, Faulkner withdrew from the university.

William Faulkner spent a year in New York City, where he worked as a clerk in a bookstore. He then spent six months in New Orleans and another six months touring Europe. The various places he visited did not seem to hold his interest for long. He was drawn back to Mississippi, to the familiar scenes and memories of his childhood. He returned to Oxford, a town full of the decaying mansions and stately magnolia trees that decorated much of the Old South.

During his wanderings and despite periods of heavy drinking, Faulkner had written some poetry and many short stories. After his return to Oxford, he continued to write, and in 1929, he published *Sartoris*. In this novel, a young aviator comes home from World War I, depressed over the death of his twin brother. *Sartoris* was the first of the many famous novels that Faulkner set in the fictional Yoknapatawpha County, Mississippi.

One novel followed another, and Yoknapatawpha grew in the imaginations of the reading public. Faulkner's stories often contained violence and cruelty, but they also described people of some dignity and humor. They dealt with the post-Civil War decline of the Old South's genteel landowner. These once rich and powerful plantation owners gradually were losing their power. Formerly landless share-croppers, both black and white, had new opportunities once slavery was abolished, and they were becoming somewhat more powerful.

Faulkner examined the old traditions that ruled southern aristocracy and looked closely and critically at the relations between blacks and whites. As he published more and more books about Yoknapatawpha County, the area began to seem almost real. William Faulkner eventually drew a detailed map of the county, identifying the important places that appeared in his stories.

In 1929, Faulkner married his childhood sweetheart, Estelle Oldham. The couple bought an old southern plantation that had been built in the 1840s, and they named it Rowan Oaks. Parts of the old house were in bad shape, and William Faulkner did much of the extensive repair work himself. The foundation was shored up and the exterior was painted; plumbing was added, along with electricity. After the restoration was complete, William Faulkner spent more than thirty years at Rowan Oaks.

Estelle and William Faulkner had one child, Jill. She remembers that "Pappy could be most difficult with adults, but he had a world of patience with children."[3] Faulkner had a lot of responsibility and many people to provide for, including his two stepchildren (from Estelle Faulkner's first marriage) and his childhood nurse, Caroline Barr.

The twenty years between 1929 and 1949 were very productive for William Faulkner. During that time, he wrote some of his most memorable books, including *The Sound and the Fury*, published in 1929. Told in four parts, the story revolves around the once-aristocratic Compson family's financial decline.

Faulkner used a style of writing called stream of consciousness in parts of his books. In this method of writing, the character's inner thoughts are presented one after another, often without the use of capital letters or punctuation. The words jump from subject to subject in much the same way that the mind moves from one topic to another. In *The Sound and the Fury*, Faulkner used the stream of consciousness technique when he wrote, "I went down the drive and out the gate I turned into the lane then I ran before I reached the bridge I saw him leaning on the rail the horse was hitched in the woods."[4]

The Sound and the Fury was followed by *As I Lay Dying* (1930), *Sanctuary* (1931), and *Light in August* (1932). In 1936, *Absalom, Absalom!* was published. It is a story about Thomas Sutpen, a poor stranger who comes to Jefferson, Mississippi, in the early 1930s to make his fortune. Faulkner describes his arrival in town: "He was already halfway across the square when they saw him, on a big hard-ridden roan horse, man and beast looking as though they had been created out of thin air."[5]

In spite of the positive reception that William Faulkner's books received from critics, none of them sold very well. In order to make some money for his family, he sometimes went to Hollywood to write screenplays. In 1948, MGM Studios paid $50,000 for the movie rights to his book *Intruder in the Dust*, a story about an African-American man who is unjustly accused of murder.

Faulkner's prestige was greatly enhanced when he was awarded the Nobel Prize for literature in 1949. He was only the fourth American to be so

Silver-haired William Faulkner was a familiar figure around his hometown of Oxford, Mississippi.

honored. In his acceptance speech in Oslo, Norway, he said:

> I believe that man will not merely endure: He will prevail. He is immortal, not because he alone among creatures has an inexhaustible voice, but because he has a soul, a spirit capable of compassion and sacrifice and endurance.[6]

Silver-haired William Faulkner was a familiar figure around Oxford, Mississippi, during the later years of his life. His niece, Dian Faulkner Wells, recalled that "his skin was weathered, tan, slightly wrinkled, and he smelled of horses and leather, cedars and sunshine, pipe tobacco and bourbon."[7]

In 1962, Faulkner's last book, *The Reivers*, was published. This is a humorous story that takes place in 1905 in Jefferson County. Eleven-year-old Lucius Priest is persuaded to steal his grandfather's car for a wild trip to Memphis, Tennessee. Lucius Priest recalls, "Grandfather's was not even the first automobile to see Jefferson or vice versa. . . . Two years before, one had driven all the way down from Memphis, making the eighty-mile trip in less than three days."[8]

Shortly after *The Reivers* was published, William Faulkner died, at sixty-five. *The Reivers* was awarded a Pulitzer Prize in 1963. After the death of William Faulkner, President John F. Kennedy said, "Since Henry James, no writer has left behind such a vast and enduring monument to the strength of American Literature."[9]

Ernest Hemingway

Ernest Hemingway
(1899–1961)

In 1918, during World War I, Ernest Hemingway tried to enlist in the United States Army. He was turned down because of poor eyesight, and he volunteered instead to drive ambulances for the Red Cross in Italy. Soon after his arrival in war-torn Italy, nineteen-year-old Hemingway transferred to the Italian infantry.

While trying to carry an injured soldier to safety, Hemingway was caught in a burst of machine-gun fire. Hundreds of pieces of metal pierced his body, especially his legs. He said later, "I blacked out. I wanted to run but couldn't, like those nightmares everyone has had."[1] When he regained consciousness, he was in a hospital in Milan, Italy. In the months ahead, twelve operations would be needed to save his legs. Hemingway's fascination with courage in the face of danger would serve as a basis for some of his most memorable books.

Ernest Hemingway was born on July 21, 1899, in Oak Park, Illinois, to Dr. Clarence and Grace Hemingway. Clarence Hemingway was a strong man who was fond of hunting, fishing, and camping. Grace Hemingway was a sensitive and religious woman who wanted her son to study music. She bought a cello for Ernest, but he was more interested in the gun and fishing pole that his father gave him.

As Ernest grew older, he liked to read and was a good student. After finishing high school, he decided against college and instead went to Kansas City, Missouri, to work as a reporter on a local newspaper. When the United States entered World War I in 1917, Hemingway could not wait to get in on the action. Even though his career in the Italian infantry was cut short by his leg wounds, the images and memories of war would remain with him for the rest of his life.

During the months that he spent in the Italian hospital recuperating, Hemingway fell in love with a nurse who was ten years his senior. After returning to the United States, he wrote to her every day, but she was not interested in the young American. Their story, along with the horrors of war, served as a backdrop for Hemingway's novel *A Farewell to Arms.*

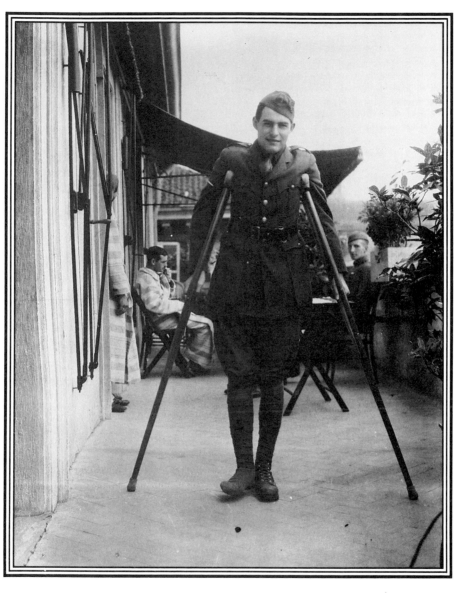

Ernest Hemingway spent several months in an Italian hospital, recovering from injuries sustained in World War I.

Back in the United States, Hemingway moved to Chicago, Illinois, where he met Hadley Richardson, a talented pianist. The couple fell in love and married in 1921. After their marriage, the Hemingways moved to Paris, France. Many other young American writers and artists, sometimes referred to as the Lost Generation, also lived in Paris during the 1920s. Among the writers was F. Scott Fitzgerald. They sat at the city's many sidewalk cafés and talked about literature, art, and the futility of war. Hemingway later said, "If you are lucky enough to have lived in Paris as a young man, then wherever you go for the rest of your life it stays with you, for Paris is a moveable feast."[2]

The Hemingways often traveled to other European countries, to get a taste of different cultures. In a visit to Spain, Ernest Hemingway attended several bullfights and was awed by the way that the matadors faced death in the ring every day. The art and mystique of the bullfight would eventually become the topic of one of Hemingway's nonfiction books, *Death in the Afternoon.*

Reality intruded on Ernest Hemingway's world when Hadley announced that she was expecting a baby. After their child, John, was born on October 10, 1923, Hemingway had to find steady work to support his family. Gone were his lazy hours in the sun as a member of the Lost Generation. Hemingway found a low-paying job as an editor and worked on his novels at home when he had the time.

All the while, Hadley grew more and more dissatisfied with her husband and with the family's nomadic existence.

Even though Ernest Hemingway's personal life appeared to be rocky, his professional life was beginning to show signs of development. In 1926, he published his first novel, *The Sun Also Rises*, a story about disillusioned young men and women in Paris, frantically trying to find happiness. *The Sun Also Rises* was a success, both commercially and critically. Suddenly, Ernest Hemingway was a celebrity, and many people wanted to find out more about him.

Pauline Pfeiffer was a reporter who was sent to interview Hemingway. The journalist and the author began to take more than a professional interest in each other, and Hemingway asked Hadley for a divorce. After the divorce was final, Ernest Hemingway and Pauline Pfeiffer were married, on May 10, 1927. The following year, the couple moved to the island of Key West, Florida. After spending the morning hours writing, Hemingway would wander around the small village barefoot, talking to the fishermen who lived in Key West. During this peaceful time, tragedy struck the family. In 1928, Ernest Hemingway's father, Clarence Hemingway, committed suicide.

In Key West, the Hemingways bought an old stone mansion that had been built in 1851. Two sons, Patrick and Gregory, were born to the couple during the following years. Because of the success of Hemingway's books, the family lived well. Ernest Hemingway indulged himself with deep sea fishing trips and bouts of drinking. By this point in his career he had sold the film rights to some of his novels, and he was widely recognized as a major American author.

Hemingway's professional success had not brought him personal happiness, though. When civil war broke out in Spain, in 1936, he rushed to the scene to report on the war. A reporter named Martha Gellhorn also was there to cover the war. They became involved, and Hemingway asked his wife, Pauline, for a divorce. Pauline Pfeiffer Hemingway remained in the house in Key West with their children. Ernest Hemingway soon married Martha Gellhorn.

For Whom the Bell Tolls, published in 1940, is based on Hemingway's experiences in Spain and Italy. In the story, an American named Robert Jordan goes to Spain to fight with a band of guerrillas during the Spanish Civil War. He falls in love with Maria, a young Spanish woman:

> She had high cheekbones, merry eyes and a straight mouth with full lips. Her hair was the golden brown of a grain field that has been burned dark in the sun but it was cut short all over her head.[3]

Five years after the publication of *For Whom the Bell Tolls*, Ernest and Martha Hemingway were divorced. In war-torn London, in 1944, Ernest Hemingway met Mary Welsh, the woman he would stay with for the rest of his life. He called her Miss Mary. The couple married on March 14, 1946, and moved to Cuba. Hemingway, who by then had a lush white beard and was known as Papa, continued to write in the peaceful atmosphere of his island home.

When asked about his writing habits, Hemingway replied, "I get up around six, six-thirty, and start work—or try to—by eight. I work until ten-thirty, perhaps even midday. Then the day's my own. I can forget work."[4]

With the passage of years, Ernest Hemingway's health began to deteriorate. His bouts of heavy drinking had taken their toll on his liver. Writing was becoming more difficult for him. Some of his critics thought that his days as an author were over. Then, in 1952, Ernest Hemingway published what many believe is his finest book, *The Old Man and the Sea.*

The story is about an old Cuban fisherman named Santiago, who has gone to sea for eighty-four days, but has failed to bring home a catch. On the eighty-fifth day, Santiago goes far out into the ocean and hooks an enormous marlin, larger even than his own small boat. Santiago battles the giant fish for two days; then he kills the marlin and lashes it to the side of his boat.

On the long journey home, sharks attack the fish, as Santiago watches:

> The two sharks closed together and as he saw the one nearest him open his jaws and sink them into the silver side of the fish, he raised the club high and brought it down heavy and slamming onto the top of the shark's broad head.[5]

In spite of Santiago's efforts to repel the sharks, they devour the marlin, leaving only a skeleton for the old fisherman to bring home.

The Old Man and the Sea sold more than 5 million copies during the first two days after its release. It reestablished Hemingway's reputation as a gifted writer who could captivate readers. In 1953, Ernest Hemingway received a Pulitzer Prize for *The Old Man and the Sea*, and in 1954, he was awarded the Nobel Prize for literature.

The Hemingways stayed in Cuba until the beginning of Fidel Castro's rise to power in the late 1950s. Fearing civil war, Mary and Ernest Hemingway left Cuba and moved to Ketchum, Idaho. There they lived on a hillside, isolated from their neighbors. Hemingway's health was poor, and he suffered several bouts of depression that required hospitalization.

Mary Hemingway, Ernest's wife of seventeen years, recalled the morning of July 2, 1961. "Yes, the shot woke me up. . . . Yes, when I found him, he was already dead."[6] Ernest Hemingway, depressed and in poor health, committed suicide just as his father had done, thirty-three years earlier.

Hemingway might have been talking about the end of his own life as he described one of his characters, Nick Adams. "He felt he had left everything behind, the need for thinking, the need to write, other needs. It was all back of him. Now it was done. He was very tired."[7]

John Steinbeck

John Steinbeck

(1902–1968)

While John Steinbeck was writing his first successful novel, *Of Mice and Men*, he made the mistake of leaving his dog, Toby, unattended for a few hours. Steinbeck said:

> My setter pup, left alone one night, made confetti of about half of my manuscript book. Two months work to do over again. It set me back. There was no other draft. I was pretty mad, but the poor little fellow may have been acting critically. I didn't want to ruin a good dog for a manuscript I'm not sure is good at all.[1]

John Steinbeck was fascinated with living creatures of all kinds. Dogs and marine life and people, especially people, were the subjects of his scrutiny and study. He wrote about America's social problems and the sorrow of its poor. He also wrote about the joy that people experienced.

On February 27, 1902, Ernst and Olive Steinbeck's only son, John Ernst Steinbeck, was born in Salinas, California, the third of four children. John's mother taught school, and his father was the county treasurer. During his elementary school years, John was interested in biology, the study of living things. He and his sister Mary spent a lot of their free time exploring the countryside.

John was a large boy, and he grew even bigger by the time he reached high school. His size was an advantage that allowed him to excel on the track and basketball teams. John also wrote for the high school paper and served as president of the class during his senior year. He liked to read and, even as a teenager, had a gift for telling a good story.

During his summer breaks, John Steinbeck held various jobs in and around Salinas. He worked on the nearby ranches, and learned about the lives of the cowboys who mended fences and branded cattle. For a time, he worked as a fruit picker in one of the many orchards that dotted the Salinas Valley. He became acquainted with the Mexican migrant workers who traveled from farm to farm, working for pennies and living in dismal conditions. He also labored with the people who ran the fish canneries that operated along the waterfront.

The working-class people that John Steinbeck

came to know during those summers would forever remain in his memory. Their stories would ferment and grow into some of his finest fiction in later years. The compassion that he felt for the plight of the migrant workers and the underclasses would one day translate itself into a masterpiece, *The Grapes of Wrath*.

After John Steinbeck's graduation from high school in 1919, he enrolled at Stanford University, in Palo Alto, California. While he was a student there, he wrote satires and poems for the school newspaper, and he took courses in writing and science.

In 1925, twenty-three-year-old John Steinbeck moved to New York City and got a job as a newspaper reporter. By 1926, he had grown tired of the East Coast, and he returned to California, where he was hired to be a caretaker at a remote estate in the High Sierras. During the long winter months, Steinbeck finally had an opportunity to devote some time to his writing. After two years in the mountains, Steinbeck's first novel was completed.

Cup of Gold, published in 1929, is a romantic tale about a seventeenth-century pirate Sir Henry Morgan. The book did not attract much attention, but it was a beginning for the struggling young writer. Steinbeck made enough money from the sale of *Cup of Gold* to permit him to marry Carol Henning in 1929. The young couple moved into a three-room cottage that John's father owned on the Monterey Peninsula.

When John Steinbeck took a break from his

writing, he often walked along the beach. In 1930, Steinbeck met a man who shared his affection for nature's wonders. Ed Ricketts owned a laboratory that supplied marine specimens to schools and research institutions. He spent his days searching for sea creatures in the waters of Monterey Bay.

John Steinbeck accompanied Ricketts on many of his collecting trips, and the two men had some memorable adventures. Ed Ricketts and his laboratory later served as a model for the story of Doc, the central character in John Steinbeck's entertaining and magical novels *Cannery Row* and *Sweet Thursday*. A passage from *Sweet Thursday* describes Doc as:

> . . . a man whose whole direction and impulse was legal and legitimate. Left to his own devices, he would have obeyed every law, down to pausing at boulevard stop signs. The fact that Doc was constantly jockeyed into illicit practices was the fault of his friends, not of himself.[2]

Doc's well-intentioned friends were a constant source of trouble for him.

Steinbeck continued to write, and the years between 1935 and 1940 were a time of success after success for the author. He wrote several major works, including *Of Mice and Men*, a story about the special friendship between two migrant farm workers, simple-minded Lenny, and George, his protector. Lenny is described as "a huge man, shapeless of face, with large, pale eyes, with wide, sloping shoulders; and he walked heavily, dragging his feet a little, the way a bear drags his paws."[3]

Steinbeck's most important work, *The Grapes of Wrath*, was published in 1939. It follows the destitute Joad family's flight from drought-stricken Oklahoma to California during the 1930s. Their search for a better life only brings them pain as they are exploited in the migrant worker camps where they look for work. Ma Joad's strength and endurance hold the family together through their suffering. "Ma was heavy, but not fat; thick with child-bearing and work. . . . Her strong bare feet moved quickly and deftly over the floor. . . . Her full face was not soft; it was controlled, kindly."[4] A great deal of controversy surrounded the publication of *The Grapes of Wrath*, for it exposed a corrupt system that preyed on the weakness of desperate people. John Steinbeck received a Pulitzer Prize for the book in 1940.

Just as Steinbeck's reputation as an author began to rise, his personal life took a plunge. In 1943, he and Carol Henning Steinbeck were divorced. Soon after, Steinbeck married Gwyn Conger, a young singer. They lived in New York during the next five years and had two sons, Tom and John. In 1948, Steinbeck's second marriage also ended in divorce, and his friend Ed Ricketts was killed when his car was hit by a train. After Ricketts' death, Steinbeck said, "There died the greatest man I have known and the best teacher."[5]

His divorce and the death of his best friend put

John Steinbeck turned out book after book during the 1950s. It was a busy time for the prolific author.

Steinbeck into a state of depression. He returned to California to live on Monterey Bay. In time, he met a woman named Elaine Scott, and in 1950, John Steinbeck married for the third and final time.

Steinbeck continued to turn out book after book during the 1950s. His stories were made into stage plays and movies, and his books were read by thousands. He had spent a lifetime writing, and in the early 1960s, he decided that it was time to take a break. Steinbeck installed a camper on the back of a pickup truck and traveled the roads of America, talking to people and listening to their stories. Beside him on the front seat of the truck rode Charley, a large black poodle who provided just the right degree of companionship during the long road trip.

When the man and the dog had finally seen enough, they returned home, satisfied. Because their experience had been so enjoyable and enlightening, John Steinbeck did the only sensible thing: He wrote about the trip. The adventure, called *Travels with Charley*, was published in 1962, the same year that John Steinbeck was awarded the Nobel Prize for literature.

In 1963, Steinbeck traveled to the Soviet Union to meet with a group of Russian writers, and he visited South Vietnam to write about that controversial war. He had suffered a series of small strokes during the preceding few years, and his health continued to deteriorate after his return from Vietnam. John Steinbeck died on December 20, 1968.

Eudora Welty

Eudora Welty

(1909–   )

In 1933, when Eudora Welty was twenty-four years old, she got a job with a newly formed government agency called the Works Progress Administration (WPA). She was paid to travel all over the state of Mississippi, checking on the status of various federal projects and writing reports on her findings. The job took her to many out-of-the-way places and exposed her to lifestyles that she had not encountered before. Welty began to take photographs of the people that she met on the back roads of Mississippi.

Through her photos, Eudora Welty began to document life in the South. She preserved on film the images of poor rural families as they laughed and as they wept. Their faces showed the harsh ravages of too much work and too little money, but they also revealed strength and pride. The impressions that Welty gathered during her Mississippi travels in the 1930s stayed with her. Those images would one day be transformed into some of the characters that populate Eudora Welty's novels and short stories.

Eudora Welty was born on April 13, 1909, in Jackson, Mississippi, the oldest of Christian and Mary Chestina Welty's three children. The well-to-do family lived in a large comfortable home that was full of books. Welty said, "I learned from the age of two or three that any room in our house, at any time of day, was there to read in, or to be read to."[1]

Eudora could read by the time she was five years old. When an irregular heartbeat kept her home from school for several months when she was about six, she spent most of her time reading. When Eudora was a little older, she visited the library often, but she was sometimes frustrated because only two books could be checked out at a time. "So two by two, I read library books as fast as I could go, rushing them home in the basket of my bicycle. From the minute I reached our house, I started to read."[2]

Eudora did not spend all of her time reading. She also took piano lessons, went to summer camp, and traveled by train to visit her grandparents. While she was a student at Central High School in Jackson, Eudora took drawing and painting lessons at a college in the area. At the age of sixteen, she entered the Mississippi State College for Women, in

Columbus. While she was a student there, she helped establish a literary magazine and was a reporter for the campus newspaper.

After two years in Columbus, Eudora Welty transferred to the University of Wisconsin, where she majored in English and earned a bachelor's degree in 1929. She then moved to New York City, to attend graduate school at Columbia University's school of business. Welty's graduate work was never completed, because she returned home after her father's death in 1931. In Jackson, she worked for a radio station and newspaper before being hired as a publicity agent for the Works Progress Administration.

Eudora Welty only held the job with the WPA for three years, but during that brief time, her outlook was altered forever. She had grown up in an upper-class home, surrounded by affection and prosperity. Through her job, Welty was introduced to the effects the Great Depression had on many of the rural poor in Mississippi. In describing a photograph that she took of an old African-American woman, Welty said:

> Her face to me is full of meaning more truthful and more terrible and, I think, noble than any generalization about people could have prepared for me or could describe for me now. I learned from my own pictures, one by one.[3]

In 1936, Welty's first story was published in a small magazine, and during the next two years, more of her work found its way into print. A collection of her stories published in 1941 received good reviews. Proceeds from *A Curtain of Green* made it possible for Eudora Welty to work full time on her writing.

The years between 1941 and 1955 were very productive for Welty. She wrote *The Robber Bridegroom, Delta Wedding,* and *The Ponder Heart,* in addition to many short stories. Her works examined, with humor and sensitivity, the relationships between people. *The Robber Bridegroom* is a fanciful fairy tale about the ravishing Rosamond. "Rosamond was truly a beautiful golden-haired girl, locked in the room by her stepmother for singing, and still singing on, because it passed the time away better than anything else."[4]

One of Eudora Welty's most notable talents was her ability to re-create the speech patterns that she heard as she made her way around Mississippi. She had a good ear for dialect and was able to duplicate it effectively. Welty's story "Petrified Man" takes place among the staff and clients in a beauty parlor. One passage relates a conversation between two of the characters: "'Reach in my purse and git me a cigarette without no powder in it if you kin, Mrs. Fletcher, honey,' said Leota to her ten o'clock shampoo-and-set-customer. 'I don't like no perfumed cigarettes.'"[5]

The Ponder Heart also takes a humorous look at southern customs and speech as it examines the murder trial of a man who is wrongly accused of killing his wife:

The State has been having themselves quite a time over a message Mr. Daniel Ponder is supposed to have sent his wife just two days before her death. If we're to rely on the word of Big John Beech, this message ran, 'I'm going to kill you dead, Miss Bonnie Dee, if you don't take me back.'[6]

Just as her skills as a writer began to grow and develop, Welty all but disappeared from the literary scene. When Eudora Welty was forty-six years old, her mother was paralyzed after suffering a stroke. In addition, both of her brothers were badly crippled with arthritis and needed help. Much of Eudora Welty's time during the next ten years would be spent caring for the ailing members of her family. She wrote and published several short stories, but she did not write any longer works during this time.

After the death of her last brother, in 1966, Eudora Welty resumed her writing career. *Losing Battles*, a story about a large family reunion, was published in 1970. It was the first of her books to become a best-seller. In 1971, Welty collected one hundred of her favorite photographs from the 1930s and published them in a book, *One Time, One Place*. All of the images revealed the various people of Mississippi, as seen through Eudora Welty's camera lens.

In 1972, *The Optimist's Daughter* was published. The book looked at the subject of grief through the eyes of a daughter who returns home to care for her father after he has surgery. His death a few weeks

In 1973, Eudora Welty earned a Pulitzer Prize for fiction with her
work, *The Optimist's Daughter.*

later brings a rush of memories to the woman as she examines their relationship. In 1973, *The Optimist's Daughter* earned a Pulitzer Prize for fiction.

As the popularity of Welty's works soared, so did the requests she received for interviews and public appearances. The governor of Mississippi proclaimed May 2, 1973, to be Eudora Welty Day in that state. In a ceremony honoring her, Governor William Waller encouraged people to read Eudora Welty's works to "find a high sense of comedy, intense tenderness, skilled characterization, and deeper insights into themselves and others."[7]

At home in the 1990s, Eudora Welty is surrounded by mountains of books, including some of those that she read as a child. Even though she has arthritis in her hands and her hearing is failing, she is still a gracious and entertaining hostess at the age of eighty-four. She continues to read voraciously the books, magazines, and newspapers that are stacked around the house on every surface. Most of her life has been lived just where it began, in Jackson, Mississippi.

In the introduction to *One Time, One Place*, Welty wrote, "Insight doesn't happen often on the click of the moment, like a lucky snapshot, but comes in its own time and more slowly and from nowhere but within."[8] Eudora Welty has had a lifetime to absorb the texture of life in her beloved Mississippi and she continues, to this day, to watch the drama unfold.

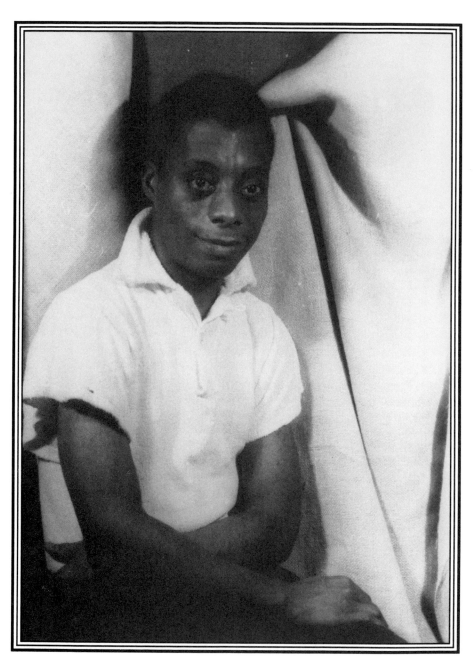

James Baldwin

James Baldwin
(1924–1987)

In 1970, James Baldwin said in an interview:

> If it hadn't been for my family, all those brothers and sisters, I'd be a very different person today. . . . So when I say that they saved me I mean that they kept me so busy caring for them, keeping them from the rats, roaches, falling plaster . . . that I had no time . . . to become a junkie or an alcoholic. The welfare of my family has always driven me, always controlled me. I wanted to become rich and famous simply so no one could evict my family again.[1]

James Baldwin was born on August 2, 1924, and he grew up in the home of his mother and step-father, Berdis and David Baldwin. The Baldwins had eight more children during the next few years and lived in poverty in Harlem, an African-American neighborhood in New York City. James spent much of his childhood caring for his younger brothers and sisters in their small apartment. His mother worked as a maid, and his stepfather was a factory worker and part-time preacher.

When James was six, he began attending elementary school at P.S. 19, in Harlem. The teachers there found James to be a good student who was interested in writing and books. They encouraged him to write, and by age nine, the young student was the author of a short play. James spent many hours with a book in one hand and a baby brother or sister on his lap. He provided comfort to the little Baldwins, and books provided comfort to James. "I read everything. I read my way out of the two libraries in Harlem by the time I was thirteen."[2]

When James Baldwin was fourteen years old, he had a profound religious experience in church and felt called upon to become a preacher, like his stepfather. Unlike his stepfather, who had a small congregation, James began to attract large crowds to his services. He had a strong voice, and his years of reading equipped him with a good vocabulary. The charismatic young preacher was more popular than his stepfather.

During the years that he preached, James also attended DeWitt Clinton High School. He was an excellent student who wrote for and edited the campus literary magazine. In his few free hours, he escaped to the movies or to a live theater performance in the neighborhood. After his graduation in 1942, James Baldwin had no hope of attending college. There simply was not enough money for tuition.

Baldwin got a job in Belle Meade, New Jersey, working in a factory that produced military materials. He encountered racial slurs and taunts in his new job and in the segregated neighborhoods around the factory. In the predominantly African-American neighborhood of Harlem, Baldwin had not been subjected to bigotry to any large degree. It was a new and disturbing experience for the sensitive young man.

While Baldwin was working in the factory, his stepfather died. Faced with the responsibility of caring for his large family, Baldwin moved to Greenwich Village in New York City to try to become a writer. Both the Village and Harlem were known as havens for artists, writers, and musicians in the 1920s.

In order to make money for living expenses, Baldwin worked as a dishwasher, handyman, and waiter. He wrote in his free time. The struggling writer became acquainted with Richard Wright, a well-known African-American author. The older man helped Baldwin get a fellowship that provided funding for his writing. Some of Baldwin's pieces were published in magazines, but his success was clouded by the continuing racism that he encountered in America. In 1948, at the age of twenty-four, James Baldwin moved to Paris, France.

Baldwin arrived in France in 1948 with only $40, and he lived in near poverty during the next few years. He lived in rundown hotels, where he spent hours writing about life in the United States:

> Once I found myself on the other side of the ocean, I could see where I came from very clearly, and I could see that I carried myself, which is my home, with me. You can never escape that. I am the grandson of a slave, and I am a writer. I must deal with both.[3]

In 1952, Baldwin's first novel, *Go Tell It on the Mountain*, was published. The book examines the problems that a young man encounters as he grows up in Harlem. In one scene, Roy Grimes and his mother, Elizabeth, are talking: "'Your Daddy beats you,' she said, 'because he loves you.' Roy laughed. 'That ain't the kind of love I understand old lady. What you reckon he'd do if he didn't love me?'"[4] *Go Tell It on the Mountain* was a success, and it helped identify Baldwin as a major African-American writer. As his popularity in the United States rose, James Baldwin returned to the United States to live.

During the 1950s, Baldwin was a popular speaker on the lecture circuit. He talked about the problems that African Americans faced in their daily lives and about their attempts to overcome racial injustice. Between speaking engagements, James Baldwin turned out one book after another. *Notes of a Native Son* was published in 1955, and *Giovanni's Room* in 1956. In 1962, *Another Country* was published, with jazz musician Rufus Scott as the central character. In one scene, "Rufus sighed and

While living in France, James Baldwin spent numerous hours writing about life in the United States.

fell back, his arms beneath his head, staring at the ceiling. . . . 'I don't know up from down. I don't know what I'm doing no more.'"[5] Full of despair for himself and his fellow African Americans, Scott eventually commits suicide in *Another Country*.

As a spokesman for racial equality, Baldwin found it natural to become involved in the civil rights movement of the 1950s and 1960s. As demonstrations in the South became more violent, Baldwin became increasingly outraged by segregation. In 1962, he wrote:

> I do not know many Negroes who are eager to be 'accepted' by white people, still less to be loved by them; they, the blacks, simply don't wish to be beaten over the head by the whites every instant of our brief passage on this planet.[6]

Baldwin worked closely with civil rights leaders to seek solutions to the problems faced by the African-American community.

The nation experienced tragedy on April 4, 1968, with the assassination of Dr. Martin Luther King, Jr., the famous civil rights leader. Soon after King's death, James Baldwin was invited to Washington, D.C., by Attorney General Robert F. Kennedy, to discuss the crisis over integration that America faced. Within weeks, Robert Kennedy also was dead, the victim of another assassin's bullet. Race riots erupted as African Americans reacted to the deaths of their leaders.

Years of turmoil, marked by sit-ins, demonstrations, and riots, followed.

By 1970, James Baldwin had had enough, and he left the United States for good, to live in France. He visited periodically, but he never lived in this country again. James Baldwin continued to write about America's problems. His words were often angry; he said that whites as well as blacks suffer in a racist climate.[7]

During his last fifteen years, James Baldwin remained in France, but he never gave up his United States citizenship. He had strong ties to America, especially to his family. Late in his life, Baldwin said, "The greatest things in my life are my brothers and sisters, and my nieces and nephews. We're all friends. They continue, in their own way, to save me. They are my life."[8]

Baldwin spent his last years in St. Paul de Vence, France, in a three-hundred-year-old farmhouse. Within its sturdy walls, the writer continued his work. He said, "I write at night. After the day is over, and supper is over, I begin, and work until about three or four A.M."[9] James Baldwin died of cancer on December 1, 1987.

To others who wished to become writers, he said, "Don't describe it, show it. That's what I try to teach all young writers. . . . Don't describe a purple sunset, make me see that it is purple."[10]

Maya Angelou

Maya Angelou
(1928–)

The year was 1931, and two small children were put aboard a train in California. Their parents had recently divorced, and the children were being sent to live with their grandmother in Arkansas. In her book *I Know Why the Caged Bird Sings*, Maya Angelou recalls that experience:

> When I was three and Bailey four, we had arrived in the musty little town, wearing tags on our wrists which instructed—'To Whom It May Concern'—that we were Marguerite and Bailey Johnson Jr., from Long Beach, California, en route to Stamps, Arkansas, c/o Mrs. Annie Henderson.[1]

Upon their arrival in Arkansas, Maya and Bailey were delivered into the capable hands of their grandmother, the owner of the only African-American general store in the town. They called her Momma, and they learned to obey her rules.

As Marguerite, who was later called Maya, and her brother, Bailey, grew older, they began to work in the store. They weighed flour and sugar for Momma's customers, figuring out what was owed. The store was a meeting place for the African-American citizens of Stamps. Their joys and sorrows were discussed as the evening breeze blew across the weathered boards of Momma's old front porch.

When Maya was seven years old, her nearly forgotten father arrived at the store to reclaim his children. He packed them into his car and headed for California. On the way, he detoured through St. Louis, Missouri, and left Maya and Bailey with their mother.

In 1936, when Maya was eight years old, she was raped by her mother's boyfriend. Mr. Freeman, as he was known to the children, told Maya that he would kill her brother if she told anyone. The frightened child finally told Bailey about the assault, and he told their mother. Mr. Freeman was arrested, tried, and convicted of the crime.

After the incident, Maya stopped speaking. Unable to deal with the silence, Maya's mother sent her children back to Momma. Even though Maya did not speak for a year, her grandmother did not give up on her. Within the security of Momma's home, the terror in the child's mind slowly began to recede, and she began to talk again.

In 1940, Maya graduated at the top of her eighth grade class. Soon after that, she and her brother moved to San Francisco, California, where their mother had gone to live. Maya attended high school, and on the night of her graduation she left a note for her mother and stepfather that read, "Dear Parents, I am sorry to bring this disgrace on the family, but I am pregnant. Marguerite."[2]

After the birth of her son, sixteen-year-old Marguerite Johnson worked at a variety of jobs to support herself and her son, Guy. She later said that Guy was the greatest gift ever given to her.

> Because, when he was small, I knew more than he did, I expected to be his teacher. So because of him I educated myself. When he was four . . . I taught him to read. But then he'd ask questions and I didn't have the answers, so I started my lifelong love affair with libraries . . . I've learned an awful lot because of him.[3]

In 1950, when Maya was twenty-two years old, she married Tosh Angelos, but the marriage ended in divorce after only two years. She began a career on the stage as Maya Angelou. During the next several years, Angelou performed as a singer, actress, and dancer, and appeared in stage productions in the United States and Europe. In 1958, she moved with Guy to New York City and joined the Harlem

Writers Guild. In addition to continuing her stage work, Maya Angelou began to write short stories and poems.

In 1961, Angelou fell in love with an African freedom fighter, Vasumzi Make, and moved to Cairo, Egypt. Even though the romance did not last, Angelou and Guy remained in Africa until 1966. At that time, they left Cairo and went to Ghana, where Angelou taught at the University of Ghana, while Guy attended college there.

One evening, shortly after Angelou's return to the United States, she met with a group of friends that included cartoonist/writer Jules Feiffer, and his wife Judy, along with James Baldwin. They sat and talked far into the night. The next day, Judy Feiffer called a publisher friend and said, "Do you know the poet Maya Angelou? If you can get her to write a book, you might have something."[4] That conversation eventually led to the publication of Angelou's first book, *I Know Why the Caged Bird Sings*, in 1970.

The book, which begins with the author's train ride to Stamps and ends with the birth of Guy, became an instant best-seller. After its publication, noted African-American author James Baldwin wrote, "This testimony from a Black sister marks the beginning of a new era in the minds and hearts and lives of all Black men and women."[5]

I Know Why the Caged Bird Sings was just the beginning of a long series of autobiographical books.

The next fifteen years saw the publication of four more books that described Angelou's rich and varied life as an actress, teacher, and poet. *Gather Together in My Name*, published in 1974, describes the author's late adolescence. Angelou's stage career in the 1950s is the setting for *Singin' and Swingin' and Gettin' Merry Like Christmas*, published in 1976. *The Heart of a Woman*, published in 1981, follows Angelou through the 1950s and 1960s and ends with her move to Africa. The last volume in the series, *All God's Children Need Traveling Shoes*, was published in 1986, and deals with the author's four years in Africa.

Concerning her writing, Maya Angelou said, "When I start any project, the first thing I do is write down, in longhand, everything I know about the subject, every thought I've ever had on the subject."[6] Her topics often include the effects of racial strife on African-American people and their triumph over tremendous odds. In addition to her autobiographies, Maya Angelou is an accomplished poet and has published several books of poems, including *Oh Pray My Wings Are Gonna Fit Me Well.*

In 1981, after living in various places in the United States and Africa, Maya Angelou accepted a professorship at Wake Forest University, in Winston-Salem, North Carolina, in the American studies department. The six-foot-tall, elegant Maya Angelou has been a popular speaker on college campuses for the past decade. Her prominence and

Maya Angelou became a popular speaker on college campuses in the 1980s.

reputation led to her appearance at the inauguration of President William Jefferson Clinton on January 20, 1993. For the occasion, Maya Angelou wrote and read a long and moving poem, "On the Pulse of Morning."

In 1993, Maya Angelou published *Wouldn't Take Nothing for My Journey Now*, a collection of her experiences and wisdom. The slim volume offers impressions and comments about the spiritual journey of Maya Angelou throughout her life. In one section, she writes, "While I know myself as a creation of God, I am also obligated to realize and remember that everyone else and everything else are also God's creation."[7]

"Our young must be taught that racial peculiarities do exist, but that beneath the skin, beyond the differing features and into the true heart of being, fundamentally, we are more alike, my friend, than we are unalike."[8]

Toni Morrison

Toni Morrison
(1931–   )

After being notified that she had won the 1993 Nobel Prize for literature, author Toni Morrison said:

> Winning as an American is very special—but winning as a Black American is a knockout. . . . Whatever you think about prizes and the irrelevance to one's actual work, there is a very distinct tremor when you win a prize like the Nobel Prize.[1]

Chloe Anthony Wofford was born on February 18, 1931, in Lorain, Ohio, the second of Rahmah and George Wofford's four children. Chloe, who was later called Toni, grew up in a home that was filled with storytelling, music, and jokes. Her parents regularly told ghost stories to their four children, and got frequent requests to tell the scariest ones again. Along with the ghost stories were tales about the myths and legends of the family's African-American heritage.

George Wofford worked at various times as a welder and a car washer. The family did not always have enough money, and struggled to survive in the difficult times before the civil rights movement. Toni's mother viewed the problems that existed between the races with some degree of optimism and believed that, in time, race relations would improve.[2]

Toni's father, on the other hand, was suspicious of all white people. His daughter later said:

> My father was a racist. As a child in Georgia, he received shocking impressions of adult white people, and for the rest of his life felt he was justified in despising all whites, and that they were not justified in despising him.[3]

Toni spent the days of her childhood in a close-knit community of African Americans in Lorain, Ohio. The residents looked after each other during times of illness and difficulty. They shared their sorrows as well as their joys and gave each other a sense of security and belonging. Toni flourished in the atmosphere of her neighborhood and graduated with honors from Lorain High School in 1949.

During her student days at Howard University in Washington, D.C., Toni Wofford became involved with the drama club and appeared in several stage productions. She developed an interest in literature and received her bachelor of arts degree in English in 1953. Two years later, she earned a master's degree in English from Cornell University. Her formal education completed, Wofford moved to Houston, Texas, to teach English at Texas Southern University. In 1957, she returned to Howard University to teach English.

Upon her return to the Howard campus, Toni Wofford met Harold Morrison, an architect from Jamaica. They married and subsequently had two sons: Harold Ford, in 1962, and Slade Kevin, in 1964. The couple was divorced shortly before the birth of Slade Kevin.

At Howard, Toni Morrison joined a writer's club that met once a month. In order to have something to show to the group, Morrison hurriedly wrote a short story about a little African-American girl who wanted to have blue eyes. The story eventually was developed into a novel and published in 1970 as *The Bluest Eye*. It was the first of Toni Morrison's works to appear in print, and the critically acclaimed book helped to establish her reputation as a serious and talented writer.

Morrison left the academic world in 1965 for New York City, to become an editor at Random House, where she remained until 1984. While she was there, Toni Morrison helped to produce *The Black Book*, which follows the lives of African Americans from the days of slavery until the 1940s. It includes a collection of photographs, newspaper

During the 1950s, Toni Morrison earned both her bachelor's degree
and master's degree in English.

clippings, and bills of sale that had been collected by Morrison and the others who worked on the project. *The Black Book* exposed Toni Morrison to a history of her people that she had not studied closely before.

While she was at Random House, Morrison read the works of other writers, but at night, after her children were in bed, Toni Morrison began to create her own fiction. *Sula*, published in 1973, was Toni Morrison's first full-length novel. A story of two African-American women and their powerful friendship, *Sula* examines the restricted lives that black women must live because of their race. In a deathbed scene, one of the women says:

> I know what every Black woman in the country is doing. . . . Dying. Just like me. But the difference is they dying like a stump. Me I'm going down like one of those redwoods.[4]

In 1977, *Song of Solomon* was published. This book describes a young man from the North, Milkman Dead, who travels to the South to find his family's fortune in the caves of Virginia. During one of his searches:

> He entered the cave and was blinded by the absence of light. He stepped back out and reentered, cupping his eyes. After a while, he could distinguish the ground from the wall of the cave.[5]

Instead of finding treasure in the form of gold,

Milkman Dead discovers the richness of his family history. *Song of Solomon* sold more than 3 million copies and remained on the *New York Times* best-seller list for sixteen weeks.

Tar Baby, published in 1981, was also a best-seller. Soon after its publication, Toni Morrison was featured on the cover of *Newsweek* magazine. *Beloved*, published in 1987, would win for Morrison the Pulitzer Prize for fiction in 1988. The book is about the life of an escaped slave who murders her baby, Beloved, so that the girl will not have to become a slave.

In a 1989 interview, Toni Morrison spoke about her choice of slavery as a topic:

> I had this terrible reluctance about dwelling on that era. Then I realized I didn't know anything about it, really. And I was overwhelmed by how long it was. Suddenly the time—300 years—began to drown me. . . . Slave trade was like cocaine is now—even though it was against the law, that didn't stop anybody. Imagine getting $1,000 for a human being. That's a lot of money.[6]

In 1989, Toni Morrison became a professor of American literature at Princeton University in Princeton, New Jersey. About her own writing, she said:

> I think long and hard about what my novels should do. They should clarify the roles that have become obscured, they ought to

identify those things in the past that are useful and those things that are not and they ought to give nourishment.[7]

Morrison's characters are often African-American women who are engaged in a struggle for freedom and self-fulfillment. In creating her fictional women, the author said that she was inspired by "huge silences in literature, things that had never been articulated, printed or imagined and they were the silences about Black girls, Black women."[8] Toni Morrison's works helped to fill in some of the blank spaces.

In 1992, *Jazz* was published. This story takes place during the Jazz Age in 1920s Harlem. Many of the characters have moved North, away from the racial problems in the rural South. Their departure from the land of their ancestors is described: "They came after much planning, many letters written to and from, to make sure and know how much and where. They came for a visit and forgot to go back to tall cotton or short."[9]

In 1993, Toni Morrison was awarded the highest honor a writer can receive, the Nobel Prize for literature. At the December 10, 1993, awards ceremony in Oslo, Norway, the Academy secretary said, "In her depictions of the world of the Black people, in life as in legend, Toni Morrison has given the Afro-American people their history back, piece by piece."[10] The sixty-two-year-old Morrison was presented with a gold medal that represented her $790,000 prize.

Toni Morrison was the eleventh American to be awarded a Nobel Prize for literature since 1901, and she was the first African American to be so honored. A Nobel Prize had not been given to an American writer since John Steinbeck received the award in 1962.

Early in 1995, Toni Morrison returned to the place of some of her fondest childhood memories. In Lorain, Ohio, a reading room at the public library was dedicated in her name. During the ceremony, Morrison said, "The Lorain Public Library was so important to me. I spent long, long hours reading." She expressed a hope that the room would encourage people to sit and read books for a little while, because in books "lies the real knowledge."[11]

Chapter Notes

Preface

1. Fred Standley & Louis H. Pratt, eds. *Conversations with James Baldwin* (Jackson, Miss.: University Press of Mississippi, 1989), p. 245.

Chapter 1

1. Stephanie Kraft, *No Castles on Main Street* (New York: Rand McNally & Co., 1988), pp. 103–104.

2. Willa Cather, *O Pioneers!*, foreword by Doris Grumbach (Boston: Houghton Mifflin Company, 1988), p. viii.

3. Anne Commire, ed., *Something About the Author*, Vol. 30 (Detroit: Gale Research, 1983), p. 76.

4. Ibid., p. 79.

5. Ibid.

6. Cather, *O Pioneers!*, pp. 26–27.

7. Willa Cather, *My Ántonia* (Boston: Houghton Mifflin Company, 1977), p. 30.

8. William Howarth, "The Country of Willa Cather," *National Geographic*, July 1982, p. 71.

Chapter 2

1. Joan Givner, ed., *Katherine Anne Porter: Conversations* (Jackson, Miss.: University Press of Mississippi, 1987), p. 160.

2. Ibid., p. 106.

3. Katherine Anne Porter, *Flowering Judas and Other Stories* (New York: Harcourt, Brace and Company, 1935), p. 7.

4. Ibid., p. 8.

5. Bryan Ryan, ed., *Major 20th Century Writers, Vol. III* (Detroit: Gale Research, 1991), p. 2377.

6. Givner, p. 137.

7. Ryan, p. 2377.

8. Ibid.

9. Katherine Anne Porter, *Ship of Fools* (Boston: Little, Brown, and Co., 1962), p. 122.

10. Givner, p. 136.

11. Charles Moritz, ed., *Current Biography Yearbook 1963* (New York: H.W. Wilson Company, 1964), p. 340.

Chapter 3

1. Jeffrey Myers, *Scott Fitzgerald: A Biography* (New York: HarperCollins Publishers, 1994), p. 5.

2. Reg Wright, ed., *Great Writers of the English Language: American Classics* (New York: Marshall Cavendish, 1989), p. 30.

3. Ibid., p. 31.

4. Stephanie Kraft, *No Castles on Main Street* (New York: Rand McNally, 1979), p. 204.

5. Ibid., p. 205.

6. F. Scott Fitzgerald, *The Beautiful and Damned* (New York: Charles Scribner's Sons, 1922), p. 192.

7. F. Scott Fitzgerald, *The Great Gatsby* (New York: Collier Books, 1992) (authorized text; originally published 1925), p. 43.

8. Wright, p. 34.

9. F. Scott Fitzgerald, *Tender Is the Night* (New York: Charles Scribner's Sons, 1934), p. 156.

10. Wright, p. 43.

Chapter 4

1. Willie Morris, "Faulkner's Mississippi," *National Geographic*, March 1989, p. 321.

2. "William Faulkner: Faith That Man Will Prevail," *Newsweek*, July 16, 1962, p. 52.

3. Morris, p. 323.

4. William Faulkner, *The Sound and the Fury* (New York: Vintage Books, 1954) (originally published 1929), pp. 197–198.

5. William Faulkner, *Absalom, Absalom!* (New York: Vintage Books, 1987) (originally published 1936), p. 35.

6. "William Faulkner: Faith That Man Will Prevail," p. 53.

7. Morris, p. 316.

8. William Faulkner, *The Reivers* (New York: Random House, 1962), p. 25.

9. "William Faulkner: Faith That Man Will Prevail," p. 52.

Chapter 5

1. Reg Wright, ed., *Great Writers of the English Language:* American Classics (New York: Marshall Cavendish, 1989), pp. 78–79.

2. Robert Andrews, *The Columbia Dictionary of Quotations* (New York: Columbia University Press, 1993), p. 667.

3. Ernest Hemingway, *For Whom the Bell Tolls* (New York: Charles Scribner's Sons, 1940), p. 22.

4. Matthew Bruccoli, *Conversations With Ernest Hemingway* (Jackson, Miss.: University Press of Mississippi, 1986), p. 83.

5. Ernest Hemingway, *The Old Man and the Sea* (New York: Charles Scribner's Sons), p. 125.

6. Oriana Fallaci, An Interview with Mary Hemingway: "My Husband, Ernest Hemingway," *Look*, September 6, 1966, p. 64.

7. "The Hero of the Code," *Time*, July 14, 1961, p. 90.

Chapter 6

1. Thomas Fensch, ed., *Conversations with John Steinbeck* (Jackson, Miss.: University Press of Mississippi, 1988), p. 36.

2. John Steinbeck, *Sweet Thursday* (New York: Viking Press, 1954), p. 13.

3. John Steinbeck, *Of Mice and Men* (New York: Bantam Books, 1979) (originally published 1937), p. 2.

4. David Wyatt, ed., *Essays on The Grapes of Wrath* (Cambridge: Cambridge University Press, 1990), p. 57.

5. Reg Wright, ed., *Great Writers of the English Language: American Classics* (New York: Marshall Cavendish, 1989), p. 56.

Chapter 7

1. Eudora Welty, *One Writer's Beginnings* (Cambridge, Mass.: Harvard University Press, 1984), p. 5.

2. Ibid., p. 30.

3. Patrick H. Samway, "Eudora Welty's Eye for the Story," *America*, May 23, 1987, p. 418.

4. Eudora Welty, *The Robber Bridegroom* (San Diego: Harcourt Brace Jovanovich, 1970) (originally published 1942), p. 32.

5. Eudora Welty, *The Collected Stories of Eudora Welty* (San Diego: Harcourt Brace Jovanovich, 1980), p. 17.

6. Eudora Welty, *The Ponder Heart* (San Diego: Harcourt Brace Jovanovich, 1985) (originally published 1954), p. 110.

7. Charles Moritz, ed., *Current Biography Yearbook 1975* (New York: H.W. Wilson Company, 1976), p. 434.

8. Eudora Welty, *One Time, One Place: Mississippi in the Depression/A Snapshot Album* (New York: Random House, 1971). p. 8.

Chapter 8

1. Fred L. Standley & Louis H. Pratt, eds., *Conversations with James Baldwin* (Jackson, Miss.: University Press of Mississippi, 1989), p. 89.

2. Ibid., p. 236.

3. Michael L. LaBlanc, ed., *Contemporary Black Biography*, Vol. 1 (Detroit: Gale Research, 1992), p. 16.

4. James Baldwin, *Go Tell It on the Mountain* (New York: Dell Publishing, 1985) (originally published 1954), p. 24.

5. James Baldwin, *Another Country* (New York: Dell Publishing, 1988) (originally published 1962), p. 61.

6. Peter S. Prescott, "The Dilemma of a Native Son," *Newsweek*, December 14, 1987, p. 86.

7. LeBlanc, p. 15.

8. Standley & Pratt, p. 89.

9. Ibid., p. 244.

10. Ibid., p. 245.

Chapter 9

1. Maya Angelou, *I Know Why the Caged Bird Sings* (New York: Bantam Books, 1993) (originally published 1970), pp. 3–4.

2. Maya Angelou, "Phenomenal Woman," *Ladies' Home Journal,* October 1993, p. 128.

3. Darlene Clark Hine, ed., *Black Women in America,* Vol. 1., (Brooklyn, N.Y.: Carlson Publishing, 1993), p. 37.

4. Ibid., p. 38.

5. Michael L. LaBlanc, ed., *Contemporary Black Biography,* Vol. 1 (Detroit: Gale Research, 1992), p. 6.

6. Jeffrey M. Elliot, ed., *Conversations with Maya Angelou* (Jackson, Miss.: University Press of Mississippi, 1989), p. 12.

7. Maya Angelou, *Wouldn't Take Nothing for My Journey Now* (New York: Random House, 1993), p. 34.

8. Ibid., p. 124.

Chapter 10

1. "Nobel Prize in Literature a 'Knockout' for Morrison, 1st. Black Award Recipient," *Jet,* October 25, 1993, p. 34.

2. Charles Moritz, ed., *Current Biography Yearbook 1979* (New York: H.W. Wilson Company, 1980), p. 264.

3. Wilfred D. Samuels & Clenora Hudson-Weems, *Toni Morrison* (Boston: Twayne Publishers, 1990), p. 3.

4. Darlene Clark Hine, ed., *Black Women in America,* Vol. 2 (Brooklyn, N.Y.: Carlson Publishing, 1993), p. 816.

5. Toni Morrison, *Song of Solomon* (New York: Alfred A. Knopf, 1977), p. 251.

6. Bonnie Angelo, "The Pain of Being Black," *Time,* May 22, 1989, p. 120.

7. Hine, p. 815.

8. "Nobel Prize in Literature a 'Knockout' for Morrison, 1st. Black Award Recipient," p. 35.

9. Toni Morrison, *Jazz* (New York: Alfred A. Knopf, 1992), p. 32.

10. "Mandela, DeKlerk Accept Nobel Peace Prize While Toni Morrison Picks Up Top Honor for Literature," *Jet*, December 27–January 3, 1994 (Special Holiday Double Issue), p. 6.

11. "A Favorite Spot," *Houston Chronicle*, January 24, 1995, p. A2.

Index

About the Author

Carmen Bredeson, a former high school English teacher, received her master's degree in instructional technology. In addition to fundraising and performing volunteer work for public libraries, Ms. Bredeson now devotes much of her time to writing. Her works for Enslow Publishers include: *Henry Cisneros: Building a Better America, Ross Perot: Billionaire Politician,* and *Ruth Bader Ginsburg: Supreme Court Justice.*